The poetry of Roy Chowdhury is replete with socio-cultural nuances, belonging particularly to the Bengali language, which is naturally delicate and tender. There is always a risk that when such culturally loaded Bengali words are translated into a vigorous code like English, it may degenerate into what American translation theorist Lawrence Venuti describes as "a second-order representation." However, Dr. Kiriti Sengupta attempts the uphill task of translating the poetry of Bibhas Roy Chowdhury in his own liberal way while retaining the quintessential spirit without merely syntactically or lexically transforming source language (SL) to target language (TL). Indeed, what Sengupta does in his magnum opus Poem Continuous is an empowering and nourishing act, an act of affirmative play, an élan vital that not only ensures the survival of Roy Chowdhury's poetry but also encourages not remaining confined in local contours and gain a world platform to speak, a lingua franca to link by targeting a global readership.

— ***Muse India***
(Tuhin Majumdar & Udayan Gautam)

Bibhas's voice pulsates with an undercurrent of passion…it is melancholic yet inflected with hope…pithy in words but loaded with sensitivity…it is a reflection of the loneliness of the poet's heart and its aches—Bibhas' poetry is enigmatic with a near-mystical aura to it as he puts into words his innermost emotions about life, love, nature and other poets. He connects with both worlds—that of matter and of spirit to find and define the meaning and balance in life. His language is fragmented at times when all he has are shards of pain to be expressed.

— ***Fox Chase Review***
(Shernaz Wadia)

Bibhas Roy Chowdhury's poems present a panoramic vision of our country: poverty-stricken India, a sense of alienation after the Partition of Bengal, fidelity of human relationships. Translator Kiriti Sengupta has tried to feel the essence of the poems, and his translation has focused on new arenas of poetry, keeping in perfect consonance with the original. A translator is a creator, and Sengupta's translations are the offspring of love's labor. Translation transcends, it makes us familiar with the outer world, and we travel across the global village with the wings of poetry.

— ***World Literature Today***
(Devika Basu)

BIBHAS ROY CHOWDHURY

POEM CONTINUOUS
reincarnated expressions

Translated by
KIRITI SENGUPTA

Foreword by DON MARTIN

HAWAKAL
NEW DELHI CALCUTTA

HAWAKAL

New Delhi | Calcutta

HAWAKAL PUBLISHERS PRIVATE LIMITED
70 B/9 Amritpuri, East of Kailash, New Delhi 65
33/1/2 K B Sarani, Mall Road, Calcutta 80

Email info@hawakal.com
Website www.hawakal.com

Cover art: Shutterstock

Cover design: Bitan Chakraborty

First edition June 2014
Second edition September 2015
10th-anniversary edition June 2024

Translation copyright © Kiriti Sengupta 2024

ISBN: 978-81-19858-84-2 (Hardback)
978-81-19858-90-3 (Paperback)

Price: INR 450 | USD 16.99

I think of life;
after the wound heals
new hair won't grow again
on the skin…

for
the great Bengali poet
Binoy Majumdar

A Literary Tour-de-Force

I was greatly honored to be asked to edit this Second Edition of *Poem Continuous — Reincarnated Expressions* by the poet Bibhas Roy Chowdhury. I had edited the First Edition, and was thankful for the opportunity to work with a poet I knew only by reputation. The First Edition was actually quite successful and was quite favorably reviewed, including in some esteemed literary journals. The book became a new benchmark in English-language Indian poetry. But something else happened. Readers were saying they wanted more. The book had hit a nerve.

When faced with this situation there are two ways to go. You can publish a new book, a sequel of sorts, or you can put out an expanded Second Edition with new material. I didn't know which way they'd go here, but I knew that the translator, Dr. Kiriti Sengupta, was looking at maybe 20 new Roy Chowdhury poems to include somewhere. I didn't hear much until one day I received the usual Sengupta email. In it he said the same thing he always says, which simply is, "Would you mind taking a look at a manuscript?" And attached was the Second Edition of *Poem Continuous.*

As I started editing I quickly became aware of how amazingly good this poetry really is! I think with the First Edition I may have not fully appreciated the quality because I was working with a new poet I hadn't worked with before. I was spending a lot of time and energy trying to get into the psyche of the man, trying to figure out who he really was and what he was trying to do. With this Second Edition I was reading it more like an ordinary reader, because I was already familiar with Roy Chowdhury's work. There really are some astounding poems here, and I enjoyed them immensely!

Like any reader I have my favorites.

The first poem which jumped out at me was "*Bhatiali—Song of the Boatmen*". I do not claim to be a student of Indian history, nor do I know all the details of the Partition of Bengal. I do understand, however, that the Partition caused deep wounds, some of which remain even today. Those wounds are expressed in this short poem, by a person who is obviously still feeling them. Such honesty (and agony) is refreshing to see in poetry, and I always appreciate it. And what to make of the last line, *Union of the parted Bengal will aid in my recovery*? I suspect that there are several interpretations of that line. I have mine. What's yours?

"Birth of a Legend" is another poem I really like. It's a rare Roy Chowdhury narrative poem, and a mystery no less! Here the poet traps us, his readers, with the early line, *Ma got a nickname: Rain.* And of course now we all want to know just how this happened. So the poet tells us a story, almost in a fable format. These kinds of poems are just fun to read because they are at first entertaining, and then you can make of them what you will. My idea of this poem may well be different than yours, but I'm certain we both enjoyed the tale!

A final poem I'll mention is "Poetry," because it reminds me a lot of my father's work (Dad was a poet who wrote under the name Saffron Bindy). One thing dad could never figure out was where his poems came from. So like any decent poet he wrote poems about writing poems. One of my favorites of his was simply titled "Words." It describes how sometimes words just randomly popped into his head, and he couldn't rest until he put them down on paper, in some sort of order that looked something like a poem. Roy Chowdhury says essentially the same thing here, with the line, *poems arrive like rumors inside the mind.* I write fiction and I think I'm fairly good at it. But I could never write poetry! It's just too mysterious, and I would have no idea how it's done.

I'll like to say the same as I had written before in the First Edition of *Poem Continuous*:

> Fortunately Dr. Kiriti Sengupta is a first-rate translator, and he has broad and deep experience with the language. Additionally, Kiriti is a best-selling poet himself, and he has a fine appreciation for the poetic art form. Who better to translate the often subtle and sometimes complex poems of a fellow Bengali poet? *Poem Continuous* is a literary tour-de-force which well-demonstrates that Bengali

poetry can, in fact, be accurately and well translated.

Kiriti has written often about his approach to translation, which differs from many translators working today. He says that a translation is more of a 'transition' than it is a literal translation. Attempting to translate word-for-word will get you into a lot of trouble with a language like Bengali. Rather, Kiriti looks at the process as a seamless transition from one language into another, and he has to keep all the nuances, such as implied meanings, subtle forms, and even flow intact as he gently transitions from one language into the other. Such an approach allows him to retain all the original meanings the poet included, as well as the underlying beauty of the language. Dr. Sengupta translates the whole gestalt of the poem, rather than just the individual words.

Poem Continuous is a wonderful introduction to the lush world of Bengali poetry. With many translations I always have the distinct feeling that I'm reading a translation. I can see, and feel, the hesitancy and the uncertainty. What has the translator left out, perhaps for expediency, which I am now missing? Not so here! This is a seamless, and highly readable, English translation of some very accomplished Bengali poetry. Experienced lovers of poetry will immediately recognize the significance and nuances of the work. Those new to Bengali poetry are in for a real treat! I would be hard-pressed to name another book of contemporary Bengali poetry quite as good as this one!

I'm sure that all readers will come to have favorite poems of their own from this collection. Poems which talk to them or have particular meanings for whatever personal reasons. And we'll each likely differ in which our favorites are. That's the beauty of really good poetry. Poems which are well-written, tightly constructed, and presented with no pretense. The best poets speak to each of us in different ways, and we each can select our own favorites, those poems we read and reread over and over, for our own personal reasons. So don't be shy! Jump right on in and find your favorites here. I guarantee you won't be disappointed!

Don Martin
September 7, 2015
Tucson, Arizona

Don Martin, an author and editor, lived in Tucson, Arizona. He wrote the widely-read column, "The View From The Streets," about issues homeless people faced. Don was also a music writer and critic (concert and CD reviews, and band interviews) and a book reviewer.

Translator's Note

"A competent translator suffers the agony
of a surrogate mother."
　　　　　—Bibhas Roy Chowdhury

Bibhas Roy Chowdhury is one of the most talented Bengali
poets, beginning in the '90s and continuing to this day. He
is a private person, however, and hates publicity. When I
was offered the chance to translate his poems into English
I was anxious, for I never had the opportunity to interact
with this poet in person. I believe that it is important to
understand the psyche of the poet in order to make the
translations live and successful. Honestly, this is a time-
consuming task, and one needs to gel quite well with the
poet to do the best with his/her published works. I can
remember that in September 2013, Roy Chowdhury gifted
me a copy of his book under the title, *Sreshtho Kobita*, which
was a collection of his memorable poems. I suggested him
to mark a few poems that he would like me to translate. He
did me the favor and said, "Carry on, brother." Since then
I have been in touch with Roy Chowdhury on a regular

basis, for whenever I had a doubt or two he has helped me spontaneously.

One of the important features of his poems is the usage of the day-to-day words. A second important feature of his work is the positioning of the words. At times they appear random as well as scattered, but they unfailingly deliver some profound emotions. Now, translating Roy Chowdhury's poems into another language has its share of risk, for most of his poems bear an underlying current of agony. Bengali is supposedly the sweetest language of the world, and there is every possible danger as one tends to translate the typical Bengali flavor. Getting into the soul of a poem is undoubtedly the most challenging task for the translator.

A few of Roy Chowdhury's poems portray the implications of the Partition of Bengal. I had to be cautious when I translated those poems, for my readers may not be well-aware of the history of Bengal. In the poem "Bhatiali," Roy Chowdhury wrote, "In the core of my heart I nurse the wounded soul carefully / Union of the parted Bengal will aid in my recovery..." His wounds are fresh even now; wounds are essentially native, and they are difficult to translate into other languages.

In the poem titled "The Offering," Roy Chowdhury has consciously acknowledged Tagore as the 'source' of Bengali poetics, and has written his concern about the survival-crisis of the budding poets. Readers may also notice that in the poem titled "Celebrating Tagore," Roy Chowdhury has shared no direct cause-effect relationship, but has wonderfully projected the implications of celebrating Tagore's birthday among the Bengalis.

Poets are essentially loners, aren't they? Well, this may sound to be an old-school thought and contradicts the present trend of performance poetry, but Roy Chowdhury is least bothered. In "Being," "Dinner," and "Beside The Tears," the reader will realize his prolonged cohabitation with solitude.

I can remember during an informal launch of the first edition of *Poem Continuous* on June 18, 2014, Roy Chowdhury offered a copy (a hardcover version that it was) to Rahul Purkayastha, one of the celebrated Bengali poets of the '80s. After a week or so, Purkayastha wrote to me:

> I am an ardent fan of Roy Chowdhury's poems. The esthetics and simplicity of his verses astound me; I lose myself completely in his lines and the mysterious rhythm they carry. I have read the translated poems, and I'm very happy to see that you have succeeded in touching the inner soul of his creations. Honestly, the soul of poetry is beyond the realms of human access, and our entire life is but a journey in the search of that soul. I am overwhelmed by the sincerity of your endeavor.

Sumana Roy, a well-known critic and poet cited one of the translated poems in an article, "Tress: Offspring, Siblings, Lovers" that appeared in *The Sunday Guardian* (October 12, 2014):

> The Bengali poet Shakti Chattopadhyay created an

entire universe of relationships around trees. Bibhas Roy Chowdhury, another Bengali poet, pays tribute to that love by using one of Shakti Chattopadhyay's most famous poems "I can, but why should I go" (translated by Jayanta Mahapatra) as the starting point. Roy Chowdhury titles his poem "I Can Leave, But Why?" (translated by Kiriti Sengupta in *Poem Continuous*), and here he writes about the fear that many plant-parents have:

I have planted a few trees.
They will survive even after my death.
I'm happy that they will shade the earth
after I leave this world.

After this is a brief catalogue about the strife and troubles of life, but it is the concluding line that holds in it the difficult temper of the parent-child relationship: "Will those plants survive even after my demise?" We, who wish a thousand year life to our human progeny, knowing the impossibility of *Jiye tu hazaar saal* (May you live a thousand years), find it difficult to wish the same for our plants. The reason behind that is the question of attention: Who will water them when I am no more?

I was curious to know if the translated verses made sense and were found readable by the readers who had no understanding of the Bengali language. I was taken aback when G. Emil Reutter sent along an invitation to re-publish a poem "Lunatic" (it first appeared in *Poem Continuous*) in their Autumn, 2014 version of *The Fox Chase Review*. Reutter not only published the translated poem, he included the Bengali original as well.

Noted academic and critic V.V.B. Rama Rao expressed his delight as he read the book:

> Literary Translation needs to be cultivated and encouraged for promoting integration and cohesion of understanding our regional literatures in our country of multitudinous languages. A provider of lift facility, the practitioner of literary translation is a unique artist. He opens up vast horizons of literary creation in languages not known to the reader by putting those in languages the reader knows … For readers like me who have no knowledge of Bengali, Kiriti's renderings into English are the next best to read and enjoy the scintillating corpus of Bibhas Roy Chowdhury's imaginative expressions. Readers of the translated texts would hear the proxy voice of the original writer. The reader knows that he is reading a translation but as a Latin cognate which has the connotation of travel. The rendering is illuminating and I have forgotten the original and there is a willing suspension of disbelief.

Professor Sunil Sharma, who is a well-known poet and critic highly appreciated the work:

> What tumbles out of the red-tinged hard covers is a fast-flowing collection of poems with a different feel and texture, and a rich and variegated Bengal, both

as a region and a cultural sensibility, as experienced internally by one of her current best poets. You are lifted directly into a collage of powerful moments, moods and landscapes by the deft poet – and equally talented poet/translator – and nothing remains the same afterwards. If already bored of the clichéd poetry in English or its effeteness or increasing self-absorption with a fragmentary self in a fractured world, sample this one coming straight from heart in cadence musical and staccato both. The poems will come alive and crackle in your hands like verbal crackers. You will never forget the sensation thereafter. Regional writings – much neglected, despite their variety and vitality and wealth – open up new vistas and newer ways of cognizing the realities around us, and, thus, changing us in the process of reading-writing.

Poetry has a limited market, and the situation is even worse with translated poetry. While translating Roy Chowdhury's new poems I asked him, "We are aware that poetry enjoys a limited readership. Don't you want to reach out to the general readers of literature? Aren't you worried from being limited to a particular section of readers?" He flashed his characteristic smile and said, "I'm aware of the facts, and I am comfortable with limited readership. Poetry is a condensed form of literature and it is not meant for all. Had I aimed to reach out to the mass I would not have written poetry in the first place. Honestly, I would only have written stories and novels which are appreciated by a large section of readers. When I write poetry I don't worry about readership; I am happy with those few people who truly appreciate honest poetry." But then marketing goes a long way in publicizing poetry. Here again Roy Chowdhury stands rooted. He inquires, "I consider poetry my existence, my religion. And I am the last person to publicize my religion. Does spirituality call for marketing?"

There are sixty translated poems in this 10th-anniversary edition, and the last poem is titled "Epitaph." One might wonder why I kept it in a collection of poems! "Epitaph" is not only a piece of writing that has been penned down by the poet in order to engrave it on his future burial plaque. "Epitaph" is the poem that marks the union of the poet with his readers. A union of two souls is referred to as Yoga, and readers are no lesser than God. As a matter of fact, the Bengali original of "Epitaph" was once highly appreciated by the distinguished Bengali poet Joy Goswami in his phenomenal work of literary criticism under the title *Gonsaibagan*. Here is an excerpt (translated by me) from the long critique by Goswami (*Gonsaibagan*, Vol. 2, pg. 193, Prativash Publications, Jan 2011):

> "Epitaph" acknowledges its readers. There is no loud invitation to them, for this poem is aware that the readers are well placed in its body. "Epitaph" is a natural rendition—a spontaneous poem that has no element of artificiality, nor does it exude a synthetic appeal. The poem denotes an ultimate state of the poet, where "I" exists and "You" exists; here, "You" points to love that the poet cherishes,

and the poem bears "My readers" as well. What a splendid thought! … An evening sets in quietly. An evening that resembles death. Subtle, and devoid of any ferocious nature of death. The final sleep lies nowhere but "in deep of the lines." What is the chief objective of a poet? To love and to bear much love in the lines. "Here lies one whose name was writ in water"—this has been engraved on the burial plaque of John Keats. Bibhas does not want to sleep in the pyre, nor does he desire to sleep in the graveyard, he rather intends to remain "in deep of the lines."

Bibhas has employed silence in "Epitaph." Blank spaces have been used as well. "Me" space, "You" space, and then "My readers." The usage of an ellipsis signifies that his stay "in deep of the lines" won't end soon. It will continue, rather. The relationship between the poet and the reader does not end as the poet dies. This relationship is dynamic! A reader who is born after the death of a poet can derive much strength and enthusiasm from the poetry of the deceased poet. Such a reader can relate to the poet. This is but the history of literature. In a cultural world that is governed by relationships that are formed through direct interactions—"Epitaph" is positioned at its extreme opposite pole.

I take this opportunity to thank the editors and their journals/magazines that published the reviews of *Poem Continuous*. Frankly speaking, we have been overwhelmed by the reviews. We understood that readers wanted to read more poems by Roy Chowdhury. Moreover, it was necessary to include an interview that I held with the poet. As you can see, this interview was first published on *Word Riot*, an online literary journal of much reputation. You will find an excerpt (translated) from his published Bengali article. These will be helpful to understand the "making of Roy Chowdhury" better.

It has indeed been my honor to have worked with Roy Chowdhury again! He is simple, accessible and oozes the feel of the man-next-door! I got to learn a lot as I worked with him. Now it is up to my readers and critics to see if they can retrieve the flavor of Roy Chowdhury's poetics in my translation.

Thank you,

Kiriti Sengupta
June 1, 2024
New Delhi

I swam across the river
as my body
floated away in the water.

I was nowhere.

The life-less frame
stood for the poet,
they meant.

Contents

The People

How can I depart?
Sorry would feel lonely then.
It needs a companion to speak with.

In disappointment,
sorry doesn't look good.

It even refuses to get angry—
all it expects
someone would patiently hear
as it speaks.

Some snivelling...
Cups of tea together for a few evenings.

How can I depart?
His words fail to cease!

Better I keep some wound
beside the coming tune.

The Small Boat

No water to share
only some infinite beggars...

Nor had I
a reason to return.

Bird...Bird...Bird...Bird...

Fetch the sky.

Now that the river dries
suits only me.

The Weather Bulletin

Holding the manuscript in mouth,
we set out in groups in an ambiguous evening.
How shall I share my experience?
The only weakness is the manuscript.

Some lips are burned by the dazzling write of light,
some quiet lanes as well—
the manuscript knows them all.

We once said, *Love you*,
as we touched the branch of the tree.
We were weeping uncontrollably—
our weakness being the manuscript.

Once there had been a fight
between the snake and the moon of the poor men,
and one turned mad as he smeared
some breadcrumbs on his frame...
Some tiny fishes died and kept floating
as some water drained into the river
from the paddy field.

The rainbow changed its stand
as the poet frowned.
It altered its direction.

The manuscript knows these all.
We are carrying it now along the dark tunnel.

In this ambiguous evening,
our dreams begin to wander around in groups,
as a revolution sets in.
Like the small ants, we keep running
in this vernacular.

How would I make you understand the feeling
a life has gathered as it saved the manuscript,
ignoring its negligible existence
and survived on the daily wages?

I don't know if you can realize
our lovers are only the weather bulletins.

Bhatiali—Song of the Boatmen

A few songs in my heart...there in the nest of the bird
a small boat in my heart...hey! I can well be the boatman.

Some anger in my heart...let me remove all fences
on either side of the border, let my blood obliterate the Partition.

An arrow in my heart...in vigil, like an archer of my vernacular,
I keep awake in the day and night, I write my eye in the poetry.

An eye in my heart...in the eyes the courageous Bengalis,
countless patriot-camps along the alphabet list.

So many broken banks...severe lightning...many cyclones,
dream-filled hearts, and melodious Bengali tone.

In the core of my heart, I nurse my wounded soul carefully,
union of the parted Bengal will aid in my recovery.

I can Leave, but Why?
for Shakti Chattopadhyay

I have planted a few trees.
They will survive even after my death.
I'm happy that they will shade the earth
after I leave this world.

This earth is my dear horse,
running for ages,
the fire is about to die.

O earth, my heart aches for you nowadays.
Men are under fire, and I can sense
the heat of destruction.

Will these plants exist even after my demise?

The Offering

for Rabindranath Tagore

Poison in the meal
of the budding poet.

O, the source,
what is on your mind?

When Will Winter Come?
for Bhaskar Chakrabarty

Hands, and some space beside
you failed to reach beyond, did you?

But a road has its destination.

I wandered around one afternoon,
I kept wandering...

Now that it seems content, I say,
Wait, let us first understand and estimate.

Hands were there, and nothing adjacent—
even a space can read and interpret.

Eternal

I know you find it difficult
to lift your face and look straight.

The brain bears it all
as there is no mortal frame.

I know tears make your love blind.
You are to speak out nonetheless.

Lift your face for once,
I'm not here
my absence is the other sky.

There is no humiliation
before the sky.

Lunatic

A quiet earth awaits formation
in every story of the water and the bridge.

You, the earth, moan aloud
like the lunatic talk with thy self.
I find you like the very touch,
or like the quiet dreams that resemble your preparation.
These grow inside your brain—silently...
I have extended my soft paws into the tunnel of scenes.
Although I was unaware of self-defense,
and to create magic in poetry, my fingers vanished
but I have shed my pride among the days that passed by.
I have noticed my figure took a spontaneous turn
only in the dark.

As I turned, I reached the land.
As soon as I turned, I felt the solitude under construction...
I tend to die;
I hide my grief as I enter into the story
of the water and the bridge.
I think of my livelihood with my eyes closed,
and a sudden jerk thereafter...
I give away numerous beings,

from my acquired brain to the earth.
With movement, as the situation demands,
they turn into nails, teeth, black wings, and cunning eyes.
They are not in motion.
I, may be...running alone...
Being desperate or I desire salvation
at time towards the water,
and towards the bridge some other time.
As I failed to control myself, I escaped.
From the middle of the story...I escaped...
In return for my fingers, I could not give myself much,
except for a few hints of my lifeline.

The Odor of Being Upset

The soul is aware of the evening
that has arrived at some distance,
and in the tune of a bird
the river has put its flow...

I will stand against death.

I pour out for the last time
a strong dose of poetry

into the body of an ancient water.

Death by Will

Wake up,
come on...
Go and see your death.

Idiot you,
spending a lifetime sitting beside the window?

Look, your death is walking, dancing,
and chewing the almonds.

Who is singing the song of rain?
It must be an ace singer

with bleeding throat?

My Darling

I was upset yesterday night.
Today, I was able to write my tears
quite early in the morning.
I continued to weep without writing in detail.
I wrote to my girl:
The day will soon arrive...
The day will soon arrive...

Let there be love for today.

My darling is like my tears,
my morning is my crazy reader.

Speaking With the Self

If you have fear
let you be scared.

If you have the drive
let you dive deep.

I'm least bothered.

We, two old mirrors,
bite each other to die.

The Connector

It makes no sense that you hurt your throat
or bleed your mouth to say—*Love you.*

You can express your love
without uttering a word.

We have been tortured,
we couldn't even say, *Love you.*

I continued to look at you
without blinking my eyes.

When I said 'we'
I meant roadside flowers, village river,
unknown birds as well.

We didn't shout to portray our love.
We remained quiet the whole life—side by side.
We refused to hate but this morning
we told the metropolis to return
from one end of the connector.

The Poetry of a Hibiscus Flower

I don't concur with anyone.

My mother stays far away—all alone,
like the coveted hibiscus flower
hidden beneath the wild grass.

My mother lost me long back.
I could not return yet because it is impossible
for men to be correct every time. Men unknowingly
commit mistakes, ridiculously turn righteous.

The hibiscus lives in solitude as expected.
Lost people do exist, more or less, in a similar way.

But I don't concur with anyone.

The Debt

My eyes fill with tears, and I remember
we learnt separation since birth
as I got drenched in the morning sunshine.

Look, your kisses fly away to the cloud,
and your hug enables a child to identify a bird.

I'm such a meager being in today's world.
A poet who does not work at all
but engages in all these.

I must wait for some more time;
the world is approaching its end on a daily basis.

I'm indebted to my tears
for this gigantic love.

The Tie of Brotherhood

Tagore himself through his music—his invite...
The Partition of Bengal...in 1905...
His music traversed all across,
originating from Jorasanko.
Tied the knots of brotherhood—*Rakhi*—
on many wrists. It was he—the Guru.

My eyes moisten as I think—
some hands joined...hands joined...hands joined...

We are finished, aren't we?
Can you hear me, Gurudev? O Tagore?
Crowd no more...no music...hands free!
Now the ties are lost, and so are the Bengalis.

The Lighthouse

You shiver in love alongside the light, you blind.

Began, thus, so many days of mine.

I didn't hold your hands, but I merged
with the solitude all alone—along with the gray river.

Beside the road stands the green deep—distinct.
I too am physical like the light.

With much thirst I run away farther,
let the danger take a small turn.

You are the candle shy, you blind.

Yes

No misery I remember
on our lips,
you brought unhesitant

the crazy sky.

The Wound

My reader, I dip into the water just for you.

You look at the vast sea, its coast...

I appear drop by drop, at some distance;
I lose my breath...I'm breathless.
Repeatedly I dip, and I surface.

You're darling, my beloved.
You can catch me perhaps...

In many congregations,
do you search for the poet's scar, wound, suppuration?

Poets and Poems

Someone has left behind
a few words today into my being.
How far should I run away?
Do I have a choice?

Into my being, as silently someone
left behind a few lines.
Today marks the time of their carriage.

I, thus, set out.
It is the same every time.
Without hunger or thirst I must move on...

I consider myself a cursed bird with broken wings;
I'll walk by my chest to reach the line
as the sky ends to meet.

The day passed by.
Approached the evening tree,
and dark sat with folded knees.

The horizon kept weeping—
make a promise, make a promise, a promise...

It has none to bank on, does it?
This is the time to make a promise.
To whom and whose words shall I give?
Impossible it seems without the dreams.

Every poem is committed to deliver a promise.

The relation keeps mum thereafter.

Bibhas—The Illumined Expression

I break my mirror to come out after every insult.
You must know, I heal my existence by my wounds.
Seasonal fragments float in the bed of solitude,
they will descend in my future writings.
I don't remember much...
Why does the insulter love the blind lane?
The morning I wrote, it lost its light
as it picked up the necessary rhythm.

Only then I tend to rejuvenate my poem
stating "the reasons of life."
My neighbors were sleeping at the dawn,
I envisioned the entire dream!
I don't remember at all
the ones who pushed light into my eyes
as the mystery unraveled.

I have been the future-poem
of much insult, and devastation.
I am not purchased by elation.

My Little Girl

I fall in love with you, O poem—
you will shatter all symbols as you wake up.
A huff on your lips, tight lipped, you are more childish,
you roll as tears, anytime.

Life is like a father.
I even tell my daughter—fight.
O poem, fight.
Forget food and water, and fight!

Ma and Her Eldest Son

I wrote a poem of my mother
and she came.

Her stories never fail to end.
Reports of our neighborhood flood,
of the trees that got drowned,
of my father and his midnight cough,
of my brother and his noise so tough.

We even report to our mother
the story of cohabiting—
our crisis with half-done poems,
both engulfing...

Ma has failing health.

The countries fail as her health deteriorates.

No amount of crisis,
not even the poems can prevent this to happen.
What shall I say to my mother—
like the way we escaped an entire turmoil,
Ma, you better sleep?

Poetry

You first scoop some portion out from within,
then consider yourself gifted.
You are exceptionally talented.

Marks of fresh wounds you would
transfer on the body of the trees—
some naked trees—
God was gone for a shower then.

You will experience an ambiguous thirst,
but it is a game of modesty.
This is but termites inside the meditating heart.
Time continues to shed as dusts...

O eternal wound, it's up to you
if you consider this poetry or not.
From my experiences, I will declare—
poems arrive like rumors inside the mind.

A few of them surface,
the rest circulate.

To My Departed Friends

At every crossroad I was lost in my thoughts.
I have been thinking about you all, every day.

Your laughter and dummy-signs
kept haunting me to make my eyes wet.
I turned blind on the road.

I could remember—
I have been demolishing the bridges repeatedly,
I was awestruck while I crossed them.

Yet, failed love does come back,
and make me cry.
I am lost again!

The Horizon

Desperately inviting
longstanding grief
one afternoon,
I place my query
before the tallest shadow:

What is poetry?

The blind bird was painting
its nest
on the water-body.

Celebrating Tagore

I know the story of the burned summer.
Why should I tell you at all?
Counting those seven stars as I heard the divine,
I found its eyes filled and tender.

What is love? Does it relax and take rest?
I won't say anything at all.

Rather I'll identify the tears to reach
the journal bought by the melancholic lass.

The Sun-Burned Ashes

for Joy Goswami

Sun, what is there beneath your dazzle?
Merely burned ashes, right?
Sun, in this birth of my being
let me enter you inside.

My poems blaze—
how much of this knows the script?
Reader, do you know I flare in your critique?

Sun, so many blind tunes ring in you;
light meets the alphabets and thus,
enters into them.

I burn, I receive light—
my fingers become exhausted!
Reader, are you aware
this is only my future and my present?

The Light

All the lines I said
promising everyday.
You know, infinite is not
a definite expression.
I remove the factual truths,
I fly them high through my eyes—
they don't have wings.

I live and I continue to
live without much ambition.

I understand as the light
touches my lips.

All the leaves of the trees
desperately await God.

Being

When I feel lonely
I get cordial to the caterpillar:
Come here, eat my leaves.

I'll stop myself
from doing the daily chores
as I see a butterfly after some time.
I would jump and squawk:
Yes, I can recognize you.

Why couldn't I become much lonelier?

The Climate

I made an earnest appeal to the tree,
affected by snowstorm:
Get up, my dear, you are absolutely fine, come on!

I stood up as well, for I needed to keep
several of my poems beneath the snow.

Poems that remained unseen.

Get up, I said,
you are to flutter your leaves
to fetch the rain,
a day after my death.

Rain that will rinse the tears.

Provocation

No matter what...I never accepted!

The moon stood along the bridge
I'm telling you, I never accepted.

The moon forcibly filled my stomach with hunger.
I never accepted, nor did I give up;
yet water arrived upon much persuasion.

I know sleepless men die
in the heart of moonlit night.

Dinner

I believe in all:
direct, or
not-so-direct beliefs.

My bodily tree is bent in sleep,
intimate with the crescent moon.

At the fag end of faith
you remain, O existence!

I continue to live.
At every twist and turn of the road
I'm hand-picked, and the world
calls it the cardinal rule.

I believe in everything.

Here is a direct belief:
a wild kiss can be referred to
as a fire-lamp.

An indirect one, on the other hand:
a glow-worm enjoys dinner between the lips.

My Country

People think I'm brave,
but I get away with
my head down.

I don't have a way out, do I?

People, who are born in a country
infested with hunger, cannot overcome
their complexities from being inferiors.

Fantasies kill.
Nothingness puts its finger
deep inside the eyes.

I wonder why this happens!
I've fed my appetite long ago
as I sold my sweat and labor.

Unfed children with their skeletal frames
haunt me in my dreams; they weep
uncontrollably and chase the fire.

I understand my country would
continue to surface even when
I have food to eat;
I'm not allowed to escape.

I sit quietly before a plate of rice.

The core of the mirror fractures....

Birth of a Legend

We overheard and understood
Ma got a nickname: Rain.

We noticed our father remained
engrossed during the monsoon;
he passed away in the last autumn.

Ma sat joyless
beside the unfueled oven.

Time passed by...

Monsoon arrived as scheduled,
yet rain failed to drop.

My sister called up: Come, O rain.
Brother said: Come, O rain.
I followed them and invited: Come, O rain.
Not even a clot of cloud was formed in the sky.

We looked at each other and rushed to Ma;
she was nowhere:

we tried to find her out...
searched everywhere, but to no avail.
We found her white drape beside the dead oven.

We hugged each other,
and cried our hearts out.

Our undressed mother;
leaving her children behind,
where did she go away?

Mysterious rain arrived
after a few days;
Ma never returned.

With Mystery

I added mystery to my words,
kept them wherever the soil appeared moist.
I was afraid—
my lines might cease to flow, anytime
and thus, I employed myself as a believer of metaphors.

Even the shadows of the trees occurred wet.
Silently I reached there:
any probability was possible between the lips.
The body didn't know if you came today—
only *maya* speaks.

All

Everything....

[*maya* is the illusion or appearance of the phenomenal world]

Soil

I'm defeated no doubt.
I return to my garden
in the morning.

I take refuge in
the gentle composure
of flowers.

I won't be public again;
I'm lost, but I get
a world of seeds.

To be alone,
absorbing the light...

I wish and write
the death of the plants
towards a new birth
while the soil remains propitious.

In the Monsoon

The algae float in the song
of my tender age.

I wonder if the river
is nearing death.

I won't ask the bridge again—
can they cross the river all alone?

In the song of my younger age,
two blind people come
across each other quite often.

Ashram—The Retreat

A connection stands still.
It is sad as the bridge collapses;
I'm said to be unattached.

I enjoy a vast sky.
My delight lies in the
endless paddy...rice.

What a mystery!
The relation stands as-is
while the involvement is called bath.

Girl

I think of you heavily,
as I lost you;
I'm overwhelmed.

Shall we meet again?
We would, I suppose.

I keep waiting,
I hug the village as closely
as I hide my tears.

You return every morning
with the right of my childhood love.

True and False for My Father

I would like to opine
(if I'm fake):
I left home due to my father.
I wandered around the streets;
I had no shelter to take refuge in.
Due to my father
I didn't have food for days.

I'll say
(if I'm honest):
after my father's demise
I found myself duty-bound
in the crematorium—
not from being his eldest son,
like an event manager, rather.

I didn't perform his last rites.
I followed no ritual
nor did I take part in the funeral.

Someone remarked:
You are indeed
an ideal communist.

A few people said:
*Your father died, but
you remain unaffected.*

I won't add a truth or lie
to describe what happened next.
My father kept haunting me
in my dreams.
No one remembers him now,
except for me:
I have no grudges against him anymore.
I saw my father with an unkempt stubble,
he appeared helpless.
In my dreams,
he had something to say...

My dreams turned unbearable.
With every passing night,
I understood the hidden message.

I brought my daughter to the riverside,
and urged: *Don't call me Baba;
call me friend. Do you understand?*

She smiled, *But why?*

I didn't bother whether she would realize it at all.
I told my daughter a few secret words—
*Fathers rule. No one forgives the faults
of a ruler! But, friends can be pardoned
for their guilt for many times in a lifetime....*

Odor

Let there be sorrow,
this is no big deal.
Let me be adorned
by the silence of grief.

I keep the smell from my past
under the shadow of the trees
like the resplendent light, which
moves around the flower-breeds.

Why are you so worried?
No loss...no win...
A solitary soul lies intimate
with the mortal being.

Monsoon

I don't want you to become alone,
no one wants to be a loner.

You would feel sad if you become one.
You may weep, you may even remember
your friend who died.

I wish you could visit Santiniketan
in the monsoon along with others.
Please don't panic at the lightning flashes;
don't say, *I like destruction*, while coming
back from the bank of Khowai river.

You would look at the holy world
again on your next birthday
with a mark of sandalwood paste
on your forehead.

I don't desire to see you too lonely.
No one can live alone here; old times
may haunt...memories may revisit.

I doubt if women can stand
the sight of the clouds.

You would need
many monsoons
to forget me....

The Chase

I know you will come here.
But I'm not sure of your direction
as you approach me.

I keep waiting;
do come,
we must meet
for once at least.

You are the killer,
I truly believe.

Hatred speaks more than love—

I know you would be here,
anytime.

Not sure of your way, though.

Ma Won't Agree

There is a pallid photograph of my father
in my mother's house.
Broken roof, gourd-shrubs, and storms...
I visit her sometimes.
I wander around her with a motto:
I wish to bring Ma
to my new house, but
she won't agree.

Ma weeps as she hugs my daughter.
Baba is dead, the mango tree does not exist,
so is the Bakul tree that died in the flood.
They perhaps safeguarded her
at every possible border.
Ma now survives with the magic of emptiness.
She protects my father's photo
from the rain with a tattered umbrella.

My daughter wipes off Ma's tears.
She says, *Granny, a few passion flowers*
have blossomed in the garden,
would you not come to our house?
Ma won't agree.

Ma would rather say, *My son has been big trouble.*
She would invariably advice my daughter,
Your father did not take care of me at all.
Ma won't stop expressing her views; she won't stop.
I sit beside my mother—mum.
I have nothing to comment on,
I experience an illusive thunderbolt in her clouds;
I'm scared—my entire being resonates with this feeling.

Much tired of traversing
the labyrinthine passage of poetry,
I see an end of the mother-son relationship;
I wonder
is there blood in my vomit?

Let me give away my reputation of being a poet.
Let me offer those few poetry books I have authored.
Ma, please accept the awards I have received
upon much persuasion. Don't refuse those days
I blazed with poetry, and please, do come and spend
your time in my new house for the rest of your life.
All deaths are indebted to the birth.

Dejection is mesmerizing.
Leaving behind the province of marked hunger,
Ma won't agree to come.
She won't come....

Breathing

There was an ambitious library—we were not sure, but a few unidentified fingers wept in the silent dark books. I was aware of such quiet breathing that oozed from the eroded pillars of language. I threw away, and thus broke the hand-wound watch, which was not running for days. The resultant words gave me a hint of death, and then a terrible grudge emerged to make me God.

I plunged into those dark books for many a time, and I picked the eyes of an entire ocean between my lips...

I can't forget the dust of that night.

Beside the Tears

Tears are beautiful,
they blur my vision and turn it blind.
There is no sound as the birds flutter wings
while flying back home;
an evening sets in for a lifetime.

Tears are decent,
they withstand all
and choke my verbal expression.
There are the bushes of Dolan Champa
on the other side of the veranda;
and the breeze arrives at the window,
as it flows over the flowers.

I knew—
it is important to turn back
for many a time in one's life,
or depression can be cured by medicines,
or you need to work hard to earn a living, my friends.

My life stood alone for ages.

I kept awake
as it was raining the whole night;

I did not write a single line.
I'm afraid if I can explain my take;
do I really understand?
I know the tears are the best accompaniments
and there is no better privacy than being in tears.

I slept beside the tears
across the entire length of the night
with no demands.

The Blaze

I'll be born such, the trees won't get hurt,
and the birds can freely fly.

I'll be born such, the ants will rejoice
in the tiny holes in earth;
the horizon is set ablaze,
no birth anywhere around.

I've no mortal frame...
The earth has its share of dust,
and the transferable odor of lonely madmen.

A river bears the moon within
as it rests over the sand.
I'll be born such, someday...

I'll be born such, like someone who has no birthday.
Like death, I'll be born eternally
time and time again.

[First published on *Literature Studio*]

SELECTED POEMS
from
BIJDHAN SANGRAHA

Poetry consumes life.
Words form concepts.

I think
void means
you are in my grip,
yet the sky in my head
refuses to quit.

The space between
the lines of a poem
isn't genuinely white.

A poet's yearning is half-
revealed. The rest is kept hidden
in the deep of the stretch.

If melancholy enters
your dream to drink
water, it means you
haven't admitted the word
thirst. The roused does not
know. Those who are in
slumber will understand.

Silently, like a slayer
I approach my old poems.

The evil tears
adhere to the skin
of my new writing.

Love takes time to evolve.
The child battles all pain to...
When a clot appears on the eye,
it is experience.

Tolerance is a profound protest.

After rinsing hands,
a murderer routinely
splashes water on the face.

Were you not aware
God was concealment?

Amid the dark,
I quietly enter from
one tree to another.
Essence stays awake
when the world sleeps.

Keeping an insane lamp,
the last bugs on the planet
remain poetry-starved.

Holding hands is easy.
Leaving them is simple, too.
All the snogs weep like stupid.
The moist grasses know—the damp
greens on the earth.

Assuming the planet's several
shadows resulted from hiding,
you held the sun in the mirror.

Shades insinuate non-attendance.

Epitaph

I said an evening should be
similar to death, didn't I?

I will remain
for some time,
in deep of the lines...

Me

You

My readers....

EPILOGUE

An excerpt from a published essay
by Bibhas Roy Chowdhury

"Here [in Bengali literature] we rarely observe the journey
of a poet from one book to his/her other ones. We tend to
categorize a poet by reading a poem or two. If you really
appreciate poetry, try to read as many poets as you can
manage and with utmost care. We need to understand the
dynamics of writing: where and how the poets set out their
journey, how they had spent their adolescence, youth and
post-youth days, what kind of thoughts they had indulged
in, and finally the last few years before their death. If you
follow them meticulously you will be able to realize their
lives, beliefs in poetry, poetic flow, reversal of stands [in
poetry], their compromises with the passage of time, and
non-compromises. In recent times I got a book published
on my translated verses [*Poem Continuous - Reincarnated
Expressions*] and I received a plethora of remarks and
reviews ... Experienced critics bring out the innermost
side of the poet through their meditating minds. A few of
them challenge the poet and negate his/her poetics, while
others greet with their appreciation ... I think, poets are not
celebrities as made by the big publishing houses; reals poets
are like the worker honeybees that mop the sky everyday.
Someone who indulges in swabbing the sky, enjoys an
infinite haven — a timeless abode!"

[Translated by Kiriti Sengupta from the original Bengali]

"Above all, the poet has to become private with his/her own writings after a certain point of time."

An interview with Bibhas Roy Chowdhury
by Kiriti Sengupta
[First published on *Word Riot* on March 16, 2015]

Kiriti Sengupta: You have read my translation of your selected thirty poems in *Poem Continuous* (First ed.). In his foreword editor Don Martin mentioned your book as "a literary tour-de-force." Do you really believe in the translation of poetry into other languages?

Bibhas Roy Chowdhury: I don't believe in translating poetry into other languages. A poem not only belongs to the poet, it belongs to the language as well. The language that a poet uses to write his/her thoughts, feelings, and reactions, has its own characteristic features like flexibility, rigidity, lyrical quality, et cetera. All these affect the construction of a poem. During translation the language changes, and as a result the translated poem differs from the original poem. Yes, the thoughts are conveyed to some extent! This is why documentary, social, and subject-based poems are most commonly translated into other languages. A poet rarely has any demands. Poetry remains localized within

102

the domain of the concerned language. However, I must admit the publishers and/or the translators who facilitate the process of translating poetry are the ones responsible for the exposure and accessibility of the poets and of their poems across the globe. Honestly, this is an appreciable task!

Kiriti: You have dedicated *Poem Continuous* to the "great" Bengali poet Binoy Majumdar. I can even remember that you have offered a copy of this book on his *Samadhi* [burial place]. I'm pretty sure most of the readers (other than your Bengali readers) have not heard much of Majumdar. They may be wondering about him being termed "great." Can you please explain your views on Majumdar?

Bibhas: Binoy Majumdar has been one of the foremost Bengali poets in the '50s. He was a professionally qualified engineer and a well-known mathematician. He served his profession only for a few years, and later he dedicated his entire life to serve poetry. A few years later he developed a psychological disorder that stayed with him until his death. He left Calcutta, and spent the rest of his life in Thakurnagar, a suburban area that is far away from the city. I was born in Bongaon, a terminal town of West Bengal, and thus I had the opportunity to remain in his touch for a considerable period of time. I have been Majumdar's intimate follower especially during his last days. I learned from him the real meaning of dedicating one's life to poetry. I have seen so many poets in my life, I have spent days and months with many of them, but Majumdar is unparalleled. He is exceptionally brilliant in his poems. I must say that his poems have influenced my writing to a great extent although I have other poets who are my favorites. Eventually I turned ambition-less. I learned to accept negligence. Majumdar's *Fire Eso Chaka* (*Come Back, Wheel*) has been exemplary! He is superlative, and let me mention a few of his lines here:

A sparkling fish
Jumps out of the water for once
Here the water looks blue
It is transparent, however
The fish dips into the water again
Seeing this humble sight
The fruit ripens, and it turns red
As it gathers the condensed sap of pain…

Now listen to this, Kiriti:

I think of life,
After the wound heals
New hair won't grow again on the skin…

And what would you remark on this poem?

…After the first-reading of a poem
If one can remain sleepy,
In trance, or may be
In a dream-like state where imaginations prevail;
After a long time
As one re-reads the poem
If like the divine lotus
Beauty, smell, and serenity can be experienced
Then all pains, dreams, and separation are worthy;
Rich in humble words like the bubbles in wine,
Poetry … your loss of attachment.

And again:

Ye story, misuse exists in the world … all along;

Kiriti: Remarkable lines indeed. Deep and profound. Well, you have been writing poetry since the '80s. What changes do you see over these decades? Don't you think poetry has now been confined merely to construction and crafting?

Bibhas: The world has witnessed major changes during the '90s both politically as well as economically. Globalization has affected our society to a huge extent. The moral values or ethics that I bore as I grew up were missing from the society as I reached my youth. Poetry of this decade has been quite loud, straight, and crafty. Poems written during this period have been soothing to our ears, but failed to stir our emotions. Thus, poetry turned as a medium of entertainment. Most of the publishing organizations supported such poems for business, but it is to be remembered that these changes occurred mainly in the poems that originated in the city or adjoining suburbs. Poetry didn't change much in other parts of West Bengal, Tripura, Assam, and Bangladesh in the '90s. I believe, poetry emerges from our lives quite helplessly. It does not render an assurance, nor does it entertain. The so-called entertaining poems are actually rhythmic manifestos of worldly pleasures. And such poets do not respect poetry, they earn a living and reputation in the name of poetry rather. Today's poet should write about the immense darkness that prevails on the other side of light. They should be pretension-less, and they must not support corruption.

My poems first appeared in literary journals at the end of the '80s although I'm known as a poet of the '90s. I was studying in my college in those days, but I could not defy the irresistible appeal of poetry and literature as a whole. I failed to complete my higher education. The entire span of the '90s was spent in poetry. In 1996, 1998, and 1999, three full-length collections of my poems were published. As soon as the "Krittibas award" [a prestigious award that spots young, promising talent, and it was primarily managed by the eminent Bengali poet Sunil Gangopadhyay] was re-introduced in the year 1997, and I was declared as one of its recipients. Honestly, I was in a trance, and I was far from self-analysis. Much later, I realized that in my poems and in the poems of my contemporary poets, our society left its booming impact, but it was only temporary. Be it love poems or poems of social relevance, they demand a proper foundation. I think, unrecognized or neglected poets who live in remote areas, or the poets, located far away from the city chaos, write poetry that is deep and profound. I can't comment on my own poems as it is not feasible on my part, but I can tell you that the poems, written by my contemporary poets who enjoyed the limelight, were popular only for a limited period of time. Poems bearing superficial protests, and worldly love/passion may entertain the general readers of literature, but the serious readers don't quite like them. In any art-form, the matter or subject is of prime importance, while stylization, or crafting is secondary.

Kiriti: Your poems mostly deal with agony and emotions. Your readers can readily identify marks of tears. Why is this agony an essential component in most of your poems?

Bibhas: I must not forget my roots. I have channelized my existence in my poems. My living in this universe…a child from a refugee family…my parents escaped from their birthplace [Bangladesh]…no scope of their return…the land they left behind turned into a new country…the place they opted as their shelter is their new country of living…

losing wealth and much property, and thus turning into full-time laborers…I was born under extreme poverty beside the terminal fences that demarcate India from Bangladesh… did we deserve this? Those who were responsible for such turmoil are often considered historical personalities, but I hate them. The whole world is now witnessing much rift within the countries. Those who fetch Partition don't suffer, it is the common people who suffer the disturbances. No doubt, I had my share of anger and disappointments that in turn reflect the tears of the helpless people. But, I would prefer using the word "quest" instead of "anger"…my quest for living. Dreams arrived in this route: in the form of words, tears, attachment to death, and finally in the form of Maya. In all respect, my life remained starved for years. Let my poetry capture the journey of the refugee boy from extreme distress to where I stand now. I have let my life to ply behind the metaphors.

Kiriti: Other than Tagore no other Bengali poet could make it to the Nobel Prize. What is your take on this matter?

Bibhas: There are certain protocols that need to be fulfilled for an award. We all are aware of the fact that why and how Tagore was considered for the Nobel Prize. In literature, there are many authors who have not been awarded the prize. We have a rich tradition here in Bengali literature, but due to the lack of efficient translators and publishers the world remains unaware of our creations. In present time many things are possible over the World Wide Web. Let the translators work upon the literary creations by Jibanananda Das, Bibhuti Bhushan Bandyopadhyay, Bishnu Dey, Tara Shankar Bandyopadhyay, Shakti Chattopadhyay, Binoy Majumdar, Shyamal Gangopadhyay, Amiya Bhushan Majumdar, et al.

Kiriti: You don't believe in marketing your books. You don't quite like promoting yourself. You rarely attend the reading sessions nowadays. You are indeed a private person. Does privacy help you in writing poetry? Aren't you bothered of being sidelined by the media?

Bibhas: I have attended a lot of seminars, and reading sessions during the '90s. In those days, I looked out for friendship and accolades. Presently, I remain focused to my poetry without wasting any more time here and there. Media looks out for the best posts, and their list changes with every passing year. Media hardly has any interest in poetry. They are focused on present-day happenings, but poetry involves eternity. Objectives of the poets differ from that of the media people. Above all, the poet has to become private with his/her own writings after a certain point of time.

Kiriti: In "*Bhatiali*–Song of the Boatmen" you wrote, *Union of the parted Bengal will aid in my recovery.* You have often said that you have emerged from the ruins of your refugee life. Partition of Bengal and homelessness have left their deep scar unto your soul. Can you please explain it further?

Bibhas: Partition of Bengal has been an integral part of our history. It has fetched much grief, distress, and uncertainty in my life. Most of the refugees have had struggled for their food and shelter. They have accepted their fate. As a poet, I have tolerated my struggle, but I refuse to accept the same. I live in the terminal town, and the securities are strict around the border, but I don't really bother. I am born in India, and my parents were born in Bangladesh. I truly wish the Partition gets obliterated. Can religion divide the river, sky, language, paddy fields, and trees? Which religion are we talking about? Our administration has compelled me to accept this Partition. My poetry registers the noise of the shoes of the security guards around the border between India and Bangladesh.

Kiriti: You have received both appreciation and flak from being a honest, and straightforward literary critic. It can be observed of late, the poets whom you have recommended to the readers are being awarded for their literary works. I'll appreciate if you say a few words on this matter.

Bibhas: I have written several articles and critiques in different magazines, and journals. Having written analytical reviews on a regular basis I have my share of reputation from being a critic. Honestly, in Bengali literature most of the editors are happy with neutral reviews. My reviews have often offended the influential writers and editors. In return I have been punished, but I carefully nurture my beliefs as far as literature is concerned. I rarely write stories and novels nowadays. I can remember that in an article I have mentioned the names of a few young poets, and now I feel delighted that they are being recognized all over in spite of the fact that they were first refused by the famous publishers in Calcutta. I'll take their names here: Nirban Bandyopadhyay, Abhimanyu Mahato, and Himalay Jana. I am proud of them.

Kiriti: I would like to know your inspirations. Can you please name the poets who have influenced your journey as a poet?

Bibhas: When I started writing poetry I was attracted to the poets of the '70s. Poets like Joy Goswami, Shyamal Kanti Das, Mridul Dasgupta, Nirmal Halder, and Debdas Acharya have their impacts upon my journey. The town where I live [Bongaon], has a good number of talented poets. Swapan Chakraborty, Moloy Goswami, Jaladhi

Halder, to name but a few. These poets have dedicated their lives to poetry, and one can hear so many inspirational true stories about their poetic endeavors. On the contrary, my contemporary poets have been mean-minded, and they consider writing as job that allows promotion from a lower rank to higher. Poets of the '90s who reside far away from the city-lights are my favorites.

Kiriti: There has been much discussion on poetry on the virtual social media, especially on Facebook. I would like to know your stand.

Bibhas: Facebook is an alternative society. It is a silent revolution. Here the users can freely share their opinions about anything and everything. This is a dream-land where governmental restrictions are negligible, except for a few countries of course! Facebook has its share of poets and their readers. I'll say, here poetry is present in search of its readers. Neglected, but talented poets of yesteryears are now present on Facebook and they are being appreciated adequately by their fans and followers. Having said that I must add nurturing poetry is extremely important, and Facebook can only compliment the tradition of poetry.

Kiriti: Thank you so much for your time and patience. I'll see you soon.

Bibhas: You are welcome, Kiriti.

[Note: The entire interview (along with the excerpts from the poems) has been translated by the interviewer.]

ABOUT THE AUTHOR

"No ambition any more. Failures have smoothed my life, and now I quietly await love... I can experience the universe."

Bibhas Roy Chowdhury was born in the year 1968, in the terminal town Bongaon of West Bengal, India. He was one of the distinguished poets of the '90s and is now an established poet in contemporary Bengali literature. His poems bear the characteristic features of the language of love, turmoil of the life of a poet, the Partition of Bengal, and resplendent light of the lost lives. Although he has received many awards, he prefers to remain private.

Wikipedia: en.wikipedia.org/wiki/Bibhas_Roy_Chowdhury

ABOUT THE TRANSLATOR

Kiriti Sengupta, the 2018 Rabindranath Tagore Literary Prize recipient, has poems published in *The Common*, *The Florida Review Online*, *Headway Quarterly*, *Dreich*, *Otoliths*, *Outlook*, *The Chakkar*, and elsewhere. He has authored fourteen books of poetry and prose; two books of translation; and edited nine anthologies. Sengupta is the chief editor of *Ethos Literary Journal*, and he looks after the English language division of *Hawakal Publishers Private Limited*, one of the leading independent presses founded by Bitan Chakraborty. Sengupta lives in New Delhi. More at www.kiritisengupta.com.